TRUMP

2024

The Road to Taking Back the White House

By

Charles Mendel

Dedication

This text is dedicated to all true Americans.

11FP Books

2020

Grover Cleveland
22nd President of
the United States of America

In 1884, Grover Cleveland, the Democrat candidate, squared off against Republican James G. Blaine for the presidency of the United States of America. Just like any election, there was name-calling and baseless accusations rather than an address of the issues. Two other parties had candidates in this race as well. None of the candidates were incumbent.

Interesting to note that California voted Republican in this race and was worth a whopping eight Electoral College votes.

Grover Cleveland scored 219 of the total Electoral College votes and 4, 874, 986 of the popular votes making him the first Democrat to win the presidency since the American Civil War.

James G. Blaine earned 182 of the total Electoral College votes and 4, 851, 981 of the popular votes.

The Greenback Party had Benjamin F. Butler in the race and he scored no Electoral College votes but did get 175, 096 of the popular votes.

John P. St. John ran for the Prohibition Party and scored zero electoral votes but did win 147, 482 of the popular votes.

Chester A. Arthur, the incumbent Republican president lost the primary to James G. Blaine. President Chester A. Arthur only became president of the United States upon the death of President James A. Garfield.

This set the stage for James G. Blaine to face Grover Cleveland for the 22nd President of the United States of America.

James G. Blaine took his campaign on the road, making many public appearance around the country. Grover Cleveland remained largely recluse, making very few public appearances.

Both campaigned on tariff reform. The Republicans favored tariffs as a means to help American based businesses. Democrats disliked tariffs, believing that tariffs hurt American farmers. However, the issues of the country were soon turned to mudslinging.

The Democrats offered Cleveland as the clean alternative to Blaine, whom the Democrats had demonized. Republicans countered with charging Cleveland for fathering a child out of wedlock about ten years earlier. The Republican slogan against Cleveland became: "Ma, Ma, where's my Pa?"

Cleveland countered with the truth. The truth was that he had an affair with the child's mother, Maria Halpin. Halpin named Grover Cleveland as the father and Cleveland agreed to pay financial support. Cleveland remained adamant that he was not sure if the child was his or not.

The Democrats came up with their own slogan against Blaine: "Blaine, Blaine, James

G. Blaine, the continental liar from Maine!"
Just like Democrats of today automatically
calling any Republican a liar. Yet the truth
was, Grover Cleveland was indeed the father
of a bastard.

Like modern politics, the mudslinging
resulting in a Democrat win. As we all know,
when policy is the only issue presented, the
Democrats have no leg to stand on.

Grover Cleveland
The 1888 Looser

Grover Cleveland ran for re-election as President of the United States of America in 1888 and failed. Cleveland won the popular vote, but lost the Electoral College.

Unlike the modern debacle, Bush versus Gore was not the first time the Electoral College elected opposite the popular vote and the 1888 race was not the first either. The first time the Electoral College voted opposite the popular vote was in 1876 when Republican Rutherford B. Hayes defeated Democrat Samuel J. Tilden with 185 to 184 Electoral College votes. The popular vote was 4, 034, 311 for Hayes and 4, 288, 546 for Tilden.

No wonder why the Democrats hate the Electoral College. The Democrats only win the popular vote with low information voters and with the help of illegal votes as they do today. Every time the Electoral College has voted opposite of the popular vote, the Republicans have favored.

Unlike the Democrats who like to say that the Electoral College failed, the truth is, the Electoral College never fails. Its purpose is ensure proper representation across a large nation of large diversity instead of large population centers having total control. The fact that the Electoral College has voted differently than the popular vote is a sign that the Electoral College is working as designed.

It should also be noted that the Electoral College was not invented by Republicans to steal elections from the Democrats. Despite what some Democrats think, the Electoral College was invented well before the Republican Party existed.

Back to the 1888 election:

At first, the 1888 election was panning out to be a repeat of the 1884 elections in that the Republicans wanted James G. Blaine to face off against Grover Cleveland again. Blaine did not want to run again and so Benjamin Harrison took the reigns.

Cleveland had set the stage for the major campaign issue with his State of the Union Address he made a year earlier. The issue was once again tariffs. Business had felt the

12

impact of reduced tariffs, which allowed foreign business to compete with American businesses. This not only hurt the American business, but also hurt the working class.

A Republican posed as a British citizen asked the British ambassador which candidate he would vote for if he were allowed to. The British ambassador replied that he favored Cleveland. The British ambassador's reply was published and used by the Republicans to show that Cleveland's ideas were favored by foreign powers.

The Democrats countered with fraud claims, saying that the Republicans paid people to move to Indiana to swing the state to the Republican vote because the State of Indiana had voted for Cleveland in the previous election cycle. However, the Democrats did not consider that Indiana voted for Harrison because Harrison was from Indiana.

Harrison not only captured Indiana from the Democrats, but he also took Ohio and New York, the home state of Cleveland.

In the end, the Electoral College prevailed and Harrison, who was also a Brigadier General in the American Civil War had won. However, Harrison had lost the popular vote.

Benjamin Harrison, Republican Party won 233 Electoral College votes and 5, 439, 853 of the popular votes.

Grover Cleveland, Democrat Party won 168 Electoral College votes and 5, 540, 309 of the popular votes.

The Prohibition Party ran Clinton B. Fisk who captured 249, 819 of the popular votes.

The Union Labor Party ran Anson J. Streeter who captured 146, 602 of the popular votes.

Grover Cleveland

24th President of

the United States of America

In 1892, the defeated Grover Cleveland decided to run for re-election as President of the United States. This is good news for President Trump. It means he can run again in 2024.

Incumbent Benjamin Harrison secured the Republican Parties nomination and engaged with Cleveland. The race was one in which a third party won Electoral College votes. Meaning that third party votes are not wasted.

Harrison's administration and the Republican controlled Congress pushed through a series of partisan measures that caused widespread upset. The McKinley Tariff Act of 1890 was one such piece of legislation that raised Tariffs to ungodly levels. This caused the middle and lower classes to become disenfranchised with the Harrison administration, claiming that Harrison only favored the wealthy elite, as the wealthy elite became the only ones able to afford foreign goods. Republicans and the Harrison administration also suffered loss of favor for allocating millions of dollars of surplus funds (when the United States Government had a surplus) to the Civil War veteran's pensions. Sadly, the Democrats as usual, used funding veterans as an excuse to attack Republicans for wasteful spending and as a result won the House of Representatives back two years before the presidential election.

James G. Blaine served as Harrison's Secretary of State but resigned so that he could run against Harrison in the Republican primary. Against all odds of multiple Republican challengers, Harrison somehow secured the Republican nomination.

Grover Cleveland had taken work at a law firm after his 1888 defeat for President of the United States. Issues surrounding silver coinage is what motivated Cleveland to run a third time for President. The Free Silver Movement advocated the unlimited coinage of silver. In 1873 Congress passed an act that omitted the silver dollar from legal tender and this upset silver miners. In 1878, the Bland-Allison Act restored the silver dollar to legal tender status and the United States Treasury was instructed to purchase between two million and four million dollars worth so silver month and turn it into coins. In 1890, the demand for unlimited silver coinage caused the enactment of the Sherman Silver Purchase Act, which increased the government's spending on silver by 50%.

Other factors then decreased the amount of gold in the United States reserves and panic ensued. Cleveland was a supported of the gold standard and he saw silver as the problem. He thus entered the Presidential race and won the Democrat primary.

Both the Republican and Democrat Parties took a moderate approach to using both gold and silver to back the value of currency. Farmers and other citizens wanted more coinage of silver. This paved the way for the Populist Party to take a hold in this election and had a running shot at winning. Former

Greenback-Labor Party presidential candidate, James B. Weaver, won the Populist nomination and gave the Democrats and Republicans a run for their money.

Neither Harrison nor Cleveland campaigned much, both mutually out of respect for Harrison's wife who was deathly ill and would die two weeks before the election.

The Democrats focused on their racism in this presidential election cycle. Their focus was on being against the Federal Elections Bill of 1890 that was designed to protect the voting rights of African Americans. The measure allowed the federal government to monitor state and local elections to ensure no vote was suppressed.

Cleveland ultimately won. Was it racism that prevailed? Was it the strong candidacy of the Populist Party? Or was it the overstepping of the Harrison administration?

Grover Cleveland, Democrat, took 277 of the Electoral College votes and 5, 556, 918 of the popular votes.

Benjamin Harrison, Republican, took 145 Electoral College votes and 5, 176, 108 popular votes.

James B. Weaver, Populist, took 22 Electoral College votes and 1, 027, 329 popular votes. He won 4 states and half of Oregon state.

The Prohibition Party ran John Bidwell who secured 270, 770 of the popular votes.

The Democrats love to use a psychology technique called the self-fulfilling prophecy. The news media put forth the idea that Hillary Clinton was going to win. The idea behind this was to discourage the Republican vote as being useless and a waste of time since Hillary was going to win. At the same time, Democrats would be encouraged to vote since they were being told to be part of the historic election of a woman to be President of the United States and the motivation of voting for the winning team.

Good thing Republicans are not mindless sheep like Democrats. Republicans turned out and voted for Trump in record numbers.

This was something that the Democrats and Hillary did not expect.

While the Democrats used super delegates to steal the Democrat primary, not only away from Bernie Sanders, but also away from the constituents, the Democrats were messing with the Republican primary. Hillary and the Democrats thought the either Donald Trump or Ted Cruz would be the easiest Republicans to beat. Hillary and the Democrats did what they could to persuade Republican voters to vote for either Trump or Cruz and sure enough, they succeeded in making Trump the Republican nominee.

Besides cheating to win the Democrat primary and stacking the deck to run against either Trump or Cruz, Hillary also ran on the coat tails of Barack Obama. As if his failed policies were loved by the American people.

Hillary Clinton went on a rampage thinking that Donald Trump would be easy prey. She had no idea that he would bring up her many illegal dealings and her many failures. Hillary was even loaded with the debate questions before hand and she still could not out do Trump. No level of cheating allowed Hillary Clinton to topple Donald Trump.

Despite Hillary Clinton's obvious issues, the new media was still trying to pull the self-fulfilling prophecy game. As the election ensued, the News Media was predicting a Hillary Clinton landslide victory. As more and more votes came in and the people saw that a Donald Trump landslide victory was going to happen, the media kept saying that Clinton was going to win by a landslide. Eventually, it was inevitable and Trump did indeed win by a landslide.

Donald Trump won 306 Electoral College votes well beyond the 270 needed to win. Hillary Clinton only secured 232 Electoral College votes. Unfortunately, the news media and Democrats cried about the Electoral College being unfair and should be done away with because Hillary won the popular vote. Of course much of that popular vote were from questionable sources.

Hillary Clinton won 65, 853, 625 popular votes compared to Donald Trump, who won 62, 985, 106 popular votes. This comes out to 48.0% for Clinton compared to 45.9% for Trump. But ... How does this compare state by state? Where did Hillary Clinton pick up such a large popular vote lead?

State	H.C.	D.T.	Win
Alabama	34%	62%	R
Alaska	37%	62%	R
Arizona	45%	48%	R
Arkansas	34%	61%	R
California	62%	32%	D
Colorado	48%	43%	D
Connecticut	55%	41%	D
Delaware	53%	42%	D
D.C.	91%	4%	D
Florida	47%	49%	R
Georgia	45%	50%	R
Hawaii	62%	30%	D
Idaho	28%	59%	R
Illinois	55%	38%	R
Indiana	38%	57%	R
Iowa	42%	51%	R

Kansas	36%	56%	R
Kentucky	33%	63%	R
Louisiana	38%	58%	R
Maine	48%	45%	D
Maryland	60%	34%	D
Massachusetts	60%	33%	D
Michigan	47%	47.3%	R
Minnesota	46%	45%	D
Mississippi	40%	58%	R
Missouri	38%	56%	R
Montana	35%	56%	R
Nebraska	34%	59%	R
Nevada	48%	46%	D
New Hampshire	46.8%	46.5%	D
New Jersey	55%	41%	D
New Mexico	48%	40%	D
New York	59%	37%	D
North Carolina	46%	50%	R
North Dakota	27%	63%	R
Ohio	43%	51%	R

State		
Oklahoma	29%	65% R
Oregon	50%	39% D
Pennsylvania	48.2%	47.5% D
Rhode Island	54%	39% D
South Carolina	41%	55% R
South Dakota	32%	62% R
Tennessee	35%	61% R
Texas	43%	52% R
Utah	27%	45% R
Vermont	57%	30% D
Virginia	50%	44% D
Washington	53%	37% D
West Virginia	26%	68% R
Wisconsin	46.5%	47.2% R
Wyoming	22%	68% R

Looking at each state, it is clear that the winner of each state won the popular vote in that state. The Electoral College elected the person who won the most Electoral College votes based upon winning the popular vote in each state. It looks like the Electoral College functioned as intended by the Founding Fathers. Most of Hillary Clinton's extra votes came from large population centers where ill informed or clueless voters cast votes.

Trump won a legitimate landslide victory despite the media mouthpiece saying the opposite.

The Trump Presidency

- Trump signed more legislation into law during his first one hundred days in office than any other president since Harry S. Truman. He did so by being able to work with Democrats even while they demonized him.

- Trump added millions of new jobs to the American economy. Even with COVID-19, the Trump economy has been strong.

- Trump succeeded in having more Americans employed than at any other point in American history.

- Half a million manufacturing jobs were created in the United States of America under the Trump administration. He brought jobs back to America that corporations had farmed out to cheaper foreign labor.

- American manufacturing has been growing at the fastest rate in more than three decades under Trump's watch.
- The Trump economic engine has been setting record rates of growth.
- Trump's economy has seen the lowest unemployment in fifty years.
- Median house hold income hit the highest level ever recorded under the Trump administration.
- Despite the media and Democrats calling Trump a racist, his policies have seen the lowest African American, Hispanic American, and Asian American unemployment rate ever recorded.
- Despite Trump being labeled a sexist by the media and Democrats, Trump's mandates have seen the lowest unemployment rate among women ever seen in American history.

- Youth wanting a job were more able to find it under the Trump administration economy than in the past fifty years.
- Veterans reached the lowest unemployment in two decades under Trump's policies.
- Americans with less than a high school education had higher employment rates than at any other point in American history.
- 4 million Americans came off food stamps as they experienced better employment opportunities.
- Vocational training opportunities dramatically increased under President Trump.
- Most manufactures had increased certainty of the future under the Trump administration.
- Retail sales kept increasing year after year with Trump's lead. Despite COVID-19, the

stronger economy and record number of employed peoples caused the economy to thrive.

- Trump signed the biggest tax cut and reforms in American history that boosted the economy dramatically. Over three hundred billion dollars surged back into the United States economy in the first quarter of these tax cuts and reforms alone.

- Small businesses, the core of the American economic engine saw its top tax rate lower than it had been in the previous eighty years.

- Trump's expert negotiating skills helped Los Angeles score the 2028 Summer Olympics. When the media tries to say Biden drove the 2028 economic success, remind everyone that it was Trump that set the stage.

- Trump was instramental for helping all of North America win its united bid for the 2026 World Cup. Again, do not let Biden steal any economic pluses in 2026 since it was Trump that set that stage too.
- Trump opened the Alaska Natural Wildlife Reserve for oil drilling, and approved the Keystone XL and Dakota Access Pipelines that helped improve the American economy, energy independence and national security.
- Trump eliminated a record number of job and industry killing regulations.
- Trump enacted regulatory relief for banks and credit unions.
- One of the biggest things was getting rid of the Affordable Care Act (Obamacare) individual mandate. The penalty on the poor who could not afford health insurance and what cause the lowest rate of true

health coverage in American history. Let's pray that the Biden administration does not bring it back and lets doubly hope that he does not bring back the prison term for those who cannot afford that was in the original draft of the Affordable Care Act.

- Despite what the Left claims, Trump has increased access to health care by providing association health care plans and short-term duration plans.
- Trump forced the cost of life saving insulin down to an affordable price.
- Through Trumps efforts, the FDA has approved more generic drug options that ever before making access to affordable drugs easier for more Americans.
- Trump negotiated with big pharmaceutical companies to freeze planned price increases and in some cases reverse planned price increases.

- Medicare was reformed under the Trump administration to stop hospitals from over charging on the drugs they prescribed saving senior citizens hundreds of millions of dollars per year.
- Trump forced through the Right-to-Try Act that allows patients with life-threatening or terminal conditions to have access to experimental drugs.
- Trump signed legislation approving six billion dollars to fight the opioid epidemic like heroin use.
- High-dose opioid prescriptions have see a drastic drop under Trump's watchful eye.
- Trump signed the Veteran's Administration Choice Act and the Veteran's Administration Accountability Act, which expanded telemedicine service, walk-in clinics, same-day urgent care, and mental health care access to veterans.

- American coal exports increased by 60% under the Trump administration.
- American oil production hit an all time high through Trump's policies.
- America became a net exporter of natural gas for the first time since 1957 under Trump's reign.
- Trump did the United States of America and its people a huge good by withdrawing from the Paris Climate Accord.
- The Clean Power plan, which would have killed the American economic engine was put to a stop by Trump.
- Trump increased military spending, thereby securing the American position as the world's largest super power and benefiting the American soldier.
- Most of the global defense has been supported by American spending while NATO allies just enjoy. Trump shifted

seventy billion dollars of the global defense spending to the NATO allies.

- Trump has caused a portion of the Air Force to become the Space Force and the sixth branch of the United States military. The United States of America will be the first power to have a Space Force.

- Trump had more circuit court judges approved than any other new administration. Again, because he was able to work across the party aisle while the Democrats demonized him.

- President Trump courageously withdrew America from the horrible Iran-Deal.

- A win for Christians and Jews in that Trump moved the U.S. Embassy in Israel to Jerusalem.

- Trump forced the Islamic terrorist holding prison in Guantanamo Bay Cube to remain open with executive order.

- Trump enforced a travel ban from Islamic nations with high terrorism to help ensure American safety.
- Trump made historic trade deals with nations around the world.
- Trump negotiated a deal with the European Union to increase American exports into the European block.
- Trump imposed tariffs on foreign steel and aluminum to increase American output and to increase national security.
- China got the first hand hit with tariff increases in response to Chinese bad trade deals and exploitation of technology.
- Trump increased vetting of foreign refuges to ensure that terrorists were not sneaking in under the guise of refuges.
- The boarder wall, as promised, began construction under Trump's leadership.

- Trump has been nominated for two Nobel Peace Prizes for his negotiations towards piece with North Korea and other powers of the world.

President Donald Trump has accomplished more in four years that any president since the founding fathers.

Joseph Biden

46th President of

the United States of America

OK! This will not be Obama round three. Joseph Biden was select by Obama to be his vice president as insurance that nothing would happen to him because Obama knew that people feared a Biden presidency more than an Obama presidency.

Biden stumbles over words like he is vomiting up alphabet soup. This cannot go well for foreign policy.

Biden is everything that the Left hated about Trump. Granted, the accusations have all been proven false to date.

Its funny that Biden has had many women accusers, but the Left's slogan of believe the woman first seems to only apply if the accused is a Conservative.

Lots of negative information about the Biden family has come out and the media has not given it any just coverage. It seems that all the Russian ties accused to Trump actually belong to Biden and other Democrats.

So the Biden presidency will be a roller coaster of lies, deception, and placation to America's enemies while distancing this great nation from her allies.

If anything, riots will lessen for the time being since riots are a weapon of Democrats. Unfortunately, it is a false calm in the storm. As soon as a Republican regains the presidency, the Democrat will resume their riots.

The Democrats have also weaponized COVID-19. Under a Biden presidency, COVID-19 will magically disappear. Some claim, why the rest of the world is in on weaponizing COVID-19. Well, the world prefers a weaker American and Trump made a stronger American. Biden promises a weaker America, so the portion of the world that wants a weaker America played COVID-19 weaponization as well.

Under the Biden Presidency, COVID-19 will start to become less and less of a health risk by summer and be of no concern by winter 2021. And Biden will be given credit for ending the pandemic with massive communist level lock downs and restrictions. Although, the real reason will be simply that COVID-19 will be de-weaponized.

Then there is the second amendment to the United States Constitution. A gun in the hand of a citizen makes them uncontrollable by their government. Democrats want to control the populace. They therefore want to take guns away so that they are the only ones who can exercise power.

At the time of this writing, the Republicans have 50 seats in the United States Senate. Unfortunately, 51 seats are needed for control of the Senate. There will be a runoff election for the two senate seats in Georgia. Fortunately, only one of the two available seats need to be picked up by the Republicans to maintain control of the Senate.

If Republicans retain control of the Senate, then things will not be that bad as many of Biden's policies can be blocked. Sadly, if the Democrats pick up both seats and the two independent seats caucus with the Democrats then all disaster will be unleashed, as the Democrats will control the Presidency and both halves of Congress. Our only hope is the Supreme Court.

Thankfully, Biden will only be a one term president. Scary though is that Kamala Harris stands to take Biden's place if something happens in office. Harris will be far worse than Biden. Happy for Obama because Obama has two people he can pass the worst president in history trophy too.

However, it is all around bad news for America.

Let us pray that God takes control of Biden
and makes him do what America needs and
not what the Democrats want to do.

Donald Trump

47th President of

the United States of America

Donald Trump can run for a second term in 2024. Grover Cleveland did it. So keep the second term of President Donald Trump dream alive.

The bad thing is, Biden will attempt to undo many of the positive things President Trump did. In 2024, Trump will need to undo Biden's policies and re-enact his policies from his first term to be able to move forward again.

Take to social media and let President Trump know that you want him to run again in 2024.

Keep reminding America that Trump is our man for the job. For the next four years, have Trump signs and flags everywhere.

Start making Trump 2024 posters for display today.

Trump took an amazing toll on so many evils in America. Keep reminding the world of all the good that he did.

Keep calling Trump as President of the United States regardless of there being a President Biden.

Remember that the Democrats stole their own primary in 2016 from Burney Sanders to nominate Hillary Clinton. The Democrats did the same to steal the election from President Trump. Biden will be an illegitimate president. Over the next four years, fight to have voter identification and a mark, such as a thumb print that ties the voter to the ballot and provides concrete proof that the person has already voted once.

Voter registration roles are a mess with people not living in an area any more, or dead still on the roles. Let us work to get these roles cleaned up so that the dead can not longer vote and the people can no longer use the ballots of ex residents.

Electronic vote counting needs to be done away with. Each election should have an election judge from each party present and each certifies the vote for who the voter cast their ballot for. Basically like how a recount is supposed to go but being done from the start. The election judges place the ballot in the correct bin together as well.

Electronics have malfunctioned on purpose and by mistake to give votes for one candidate to another. Software has also miscalculated on purpose and by mistake.

Mail in voting is too ripe for fraud to occur. We all saw videos of postal workers throwing ballots in the trash. Not only that, but people can easily sell their vote to another or mail can be intercepted and votes cast in someone else's name. Weaponized COVID-19 is what allowed the Democrats to use mail in voting.

Democrats like to bus their voters to the polls. Maybe its time the Republicans did the same. Go get every poor voter that votes Republican and get them to the polls.

Educate the voters. Many vote based upon knee jerk reactions instead of proper education. Educate the people. Fight to make it required that a certain demonstration of competency is needed before a person is allowed to vote. After all, an educated voter rarely votes democrat.

We all have a lot of work a head of us if we want to see Donald Trump, the 47th President of the United States.

Bidenisms

Let us take a look as some of the things Joseph Biden as said over the years.

- Integrating black students would turn schools into 'A jungle… a racial jungle.
- I don't want my children to grow up in a jungle, a racial jungle.
- Well, I tell you what, if you have a problem figuring out whether you're for me or Trump, then you ain't black.
- You got the first mainstream African American who is articulate and bright and clean and a nice-looking guy. I mean, that's a storybook, man. (This was about Barock Obama).
- Unlike the African-American community, with notable exceptions, the Latino community is an incredibly diverse

community with incredibly diverse attitudes about different things.

- In Delaware, the largest growth in population is Indian-Americans moving from India. You cannot go to a 7-Eleven or a Dunkin' Donuts unless you have a slight Indian accent.

- For a woman to come forward in the glaring light of focus, nationally, you've got to start off with the presumption that at least the essence of what she's talking about is real. (Unless it is the eight or so women that have accused Biden or any woman that accuses someone on the Left).

- We choose science of fiction, hope over fear, and unity over division. (Yet in the Obama administration they chose fear over science, fear over hope, and racial and gender division over unity).

- If you were a quarter master you can sure
  in hell take care of running a you know
  department store uh thing you know were
  in the second floor of the ladies department
  you know what I mean. (And this is
  supposed to speak to foreign powers on
  behalf of the United States of America.
- We are living through a battle for the soul
  of this nation. (Satan is always looking for
  souls).
- Who rips families apart at the boarder.
  (This is in reference to President Trump but
  old Joe Biden forgets he and his buddy
  Obama were doing this and Trump had no
  choice but to carry out the law the
  Obama/Biden administration set up).
- If you elect me, your taxes are going to be
  raised not cut. (I guess no one paid
  attention to him but they will feel it in their
  smaller pay checks).

The number of Biden quotes that are pure giberish are extremely numerous. An entire volume could be written on just Biden giberish. Even a whole language could be developed from Biden giberish.

Trumpisms

- Make America Great Again. (He sure was getting the job done).

- This election was a fraud. (It absolutely was. The Democrats keep getting bolder in their cheating methods and they have been getting better at it. The very fact that Trump votes were seen thrown away by a postal worker is enough to call a new election. Especially knowing there were multiple occurances of such and knowing that the ones that were caught were just the tip of the iceberg).

- There is NO WAY Biden got 80,000,000 votes!!! This was a 100% RIGGED ELECTION. (It is statistically impossible for Biden to have gotten that many votes).

- Joe Biden was a total disaster in handling the H1N1 Swine Flu. (Remember Biden's claim to pandemic expertise was the stupidity of letting ebola infected people into the United States of America).

- ANTIFA SCUM ran for the hills today when they tried attacking the people at the Trump Rally, because those people aggressively fought back. (Just goes to show who the tough people are. Certainly not the sissy Left. But let us not forget that Hilter, Mao, and other mass murdering dictators were all on the political Left).

- As president, I will establish the national goal of providing school choice to every American child living in poverty. (The Left definitely does not want this. Truly educated people do not vote Democrat unless they use the Democrat engine to suppress others to get richer).

- I have been consistent in my opposition to Common Core. Get rid of Common Core. (Common Core has only served to confuse young minds just how the Democrats want their voters).

- If he is elected, the stock market will crash. (This is absolutely true. Biden will crash the economy so hard that it will rival The Great Depression. Problem is, is that Democrats and all of the Left will say Biden inherited the disaster from Trump while not admitting that his COVID policies and Green New deal crud are the real cause).

Remember: TRUMP 2024!!!

Fight the corruption of the 2024 election now!!!

Expose the Left now!!!

Take over the media now!!!

Create better and louder alternate media now!!!

Make voter ID required now!!!

Clean up the voter registries now!!!

Improve the integrity of the election judges now!!!

Remind the world what the Democrats really
are now!!!

Fight hard for Trump 2024!!!

www.ingramcontent.com/pod-product-compliance
Lightning Source LLC
Chambersburg PA
CBHW061523250726

48657CB00005B/2035